UP IN THE AIR

Distributed in the United States by
Smart Apple Media
1980 Lookout Drive
North Mankato, MN 56003

Text copyright © Philip Ardagh

Series devised by Philip Ardagh

Philip Ardagh asserts his moral right to be
identified as the author of this work.

ISBN 1-931983-03-8

Library of Congress Control Number: 2002 141311

Printed by South China Printing Co. Ltd., Hong Kong

Editor: Honor Head
Designer: Simeen Karim
Illustrator: Tig Sutton

UP IN
THE AIR

By Philip Ardagh
Illustrated by Tig Sutton

Thameside Press

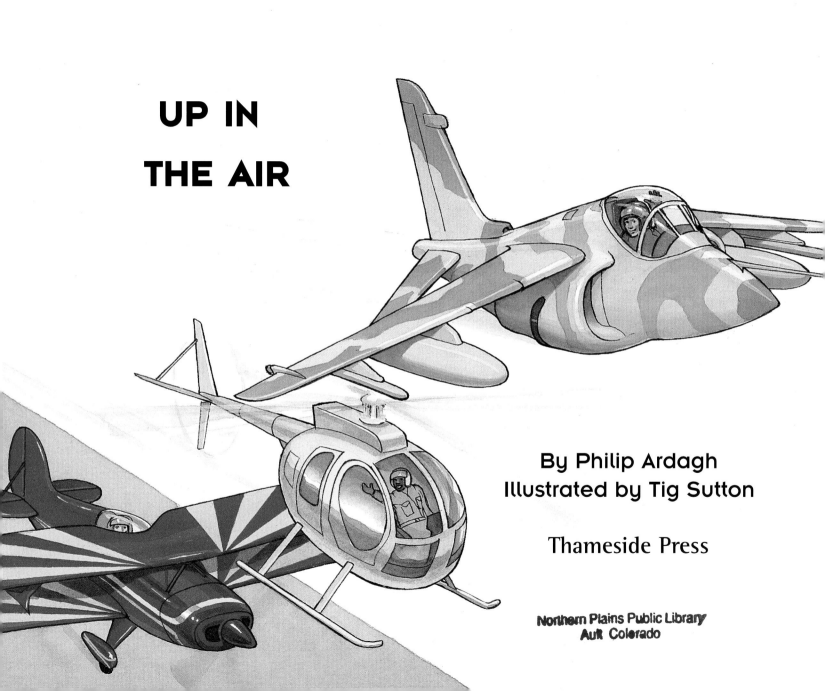

There is an airshow at the airport today.

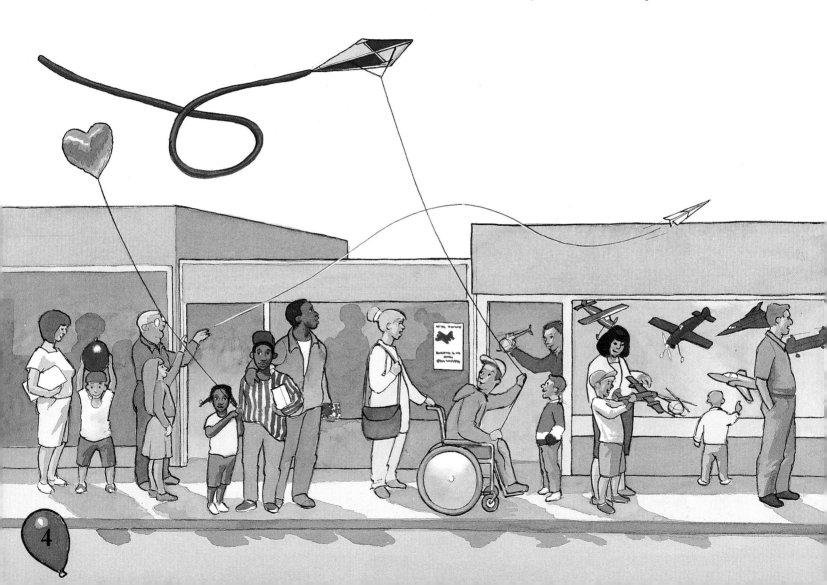

4

Up in the air, a biplane flies out of the clouds.

It pulls a banner behind it
with a message to the crowd.

6

On the ground below, a balloon is filled with hot air.

WELCOME TO THE AIRSHOW

7

When the
balloon is full,
it lifts the basket
up in the air.

A small plane speeds down the runway.

9

It takes to the sky
and loops-the-loop.

A helicopter takes off, its rotor blades spinning. It lifts up a net.

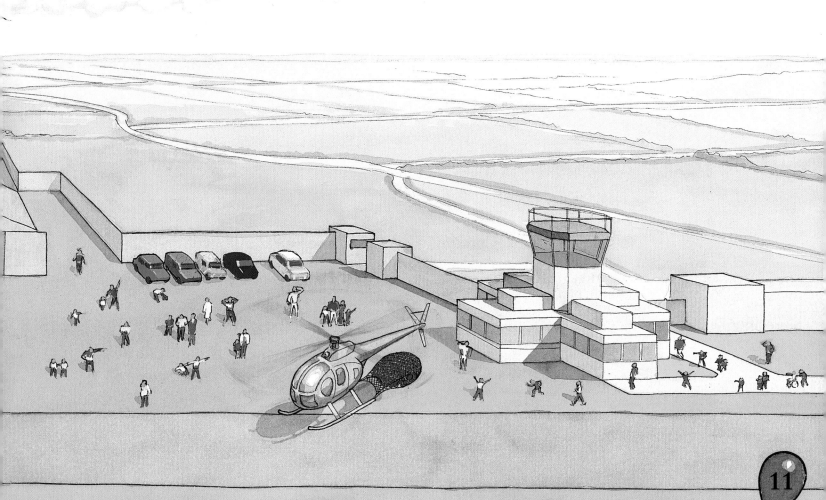

The net opens and streams of
balloons drift over the airfield.

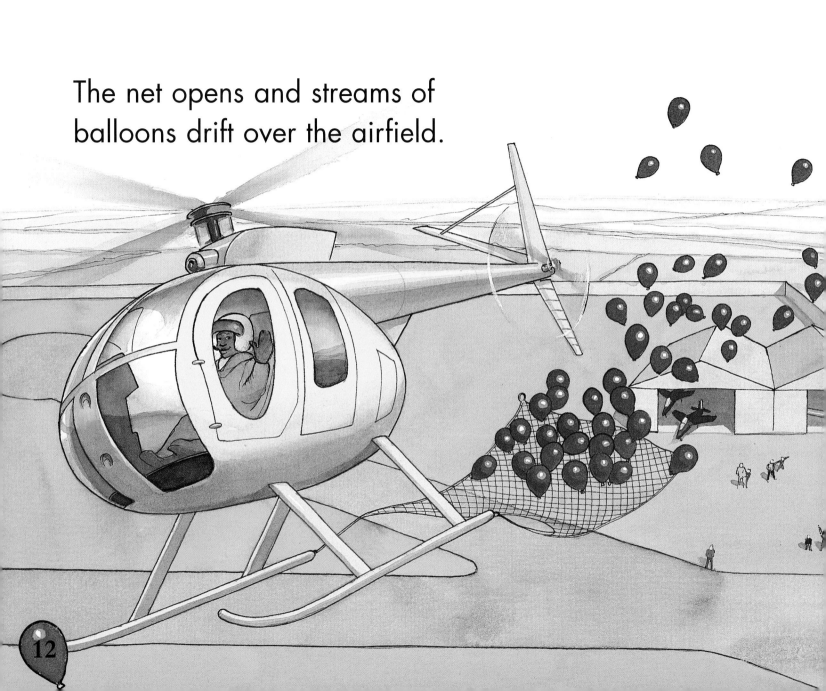

12

Concorde arrives. It speeds through the sky.

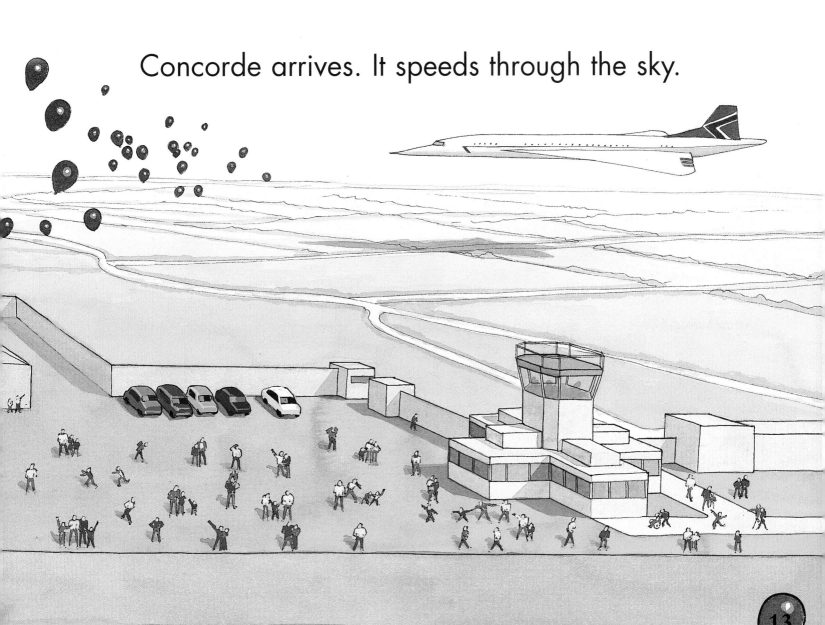

Its nose bends and it comes in to land.

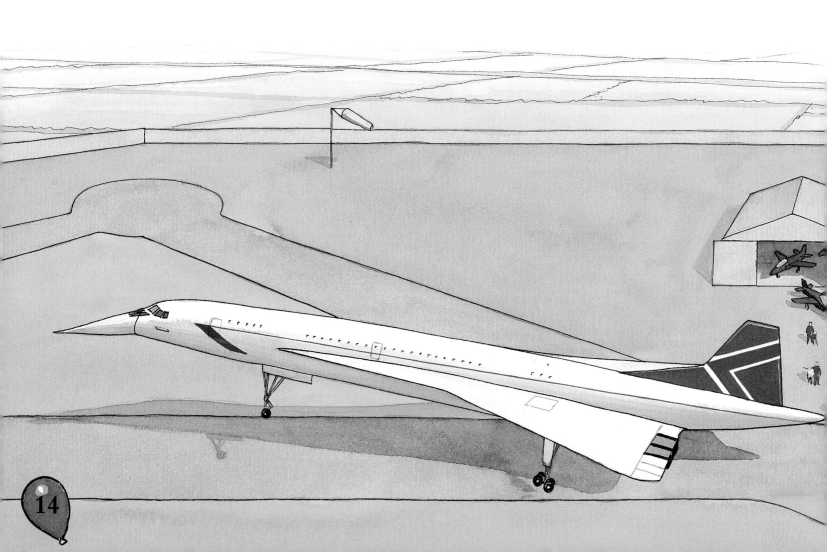

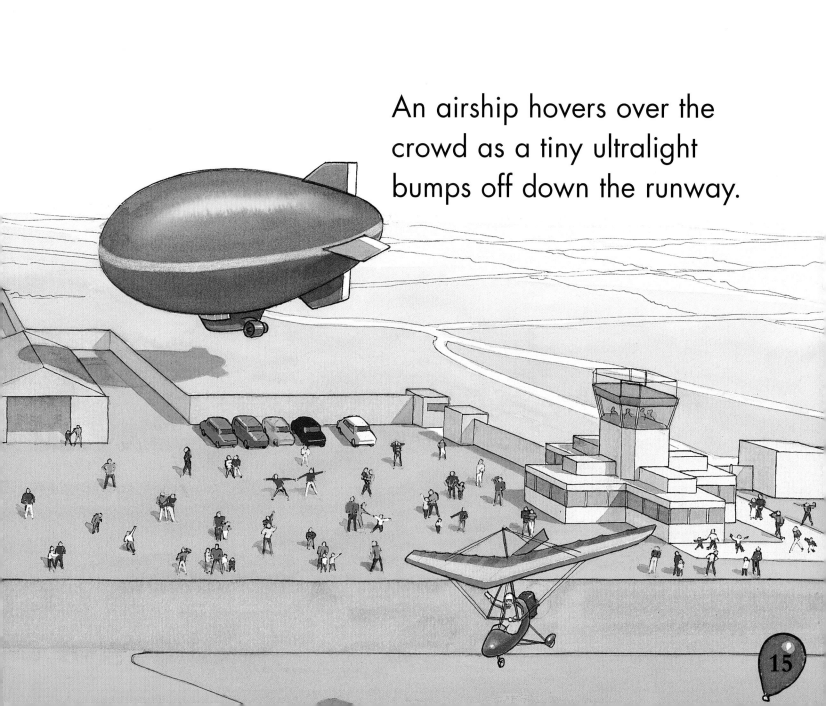

An airship hovers over the crowd as a tiny ultralight bumps off down the runway.

15

The pilot waves to the crowd.

16

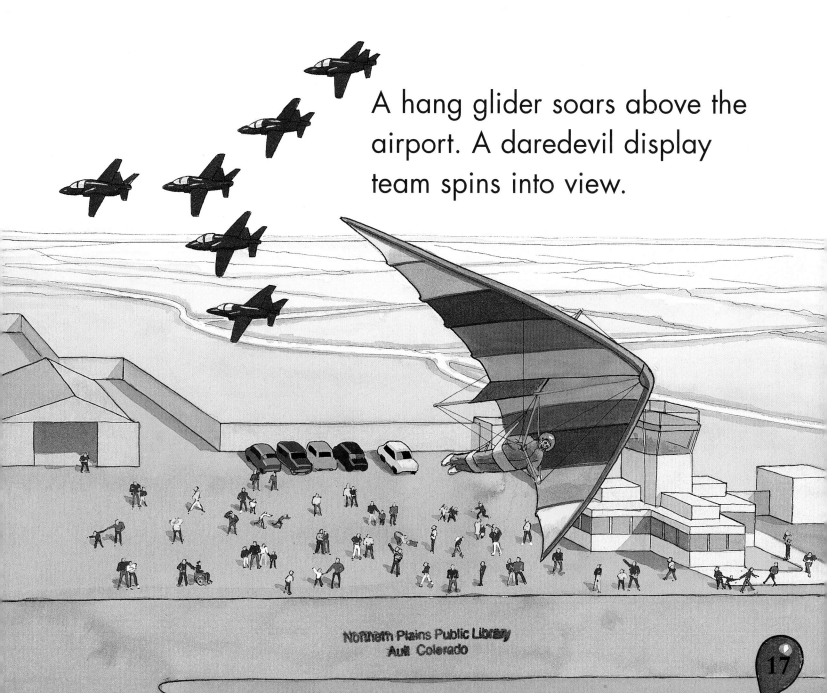

A hang glider soars above the airport. A daredevil display team spins into view.

17

Colored smoke pours from their tails as the planes spin and weave in the air.

A giant helicopter takes off from the runway.

19

Up in the air,
four sky divers
jump out.

20

A jump jet lifts off the ground.

21

It roars through the sky past a huge
jumbo jet full of passengers.

The sky divers open their parachutes and drift down to the ground.

23

A final fly-past ends the airshow.

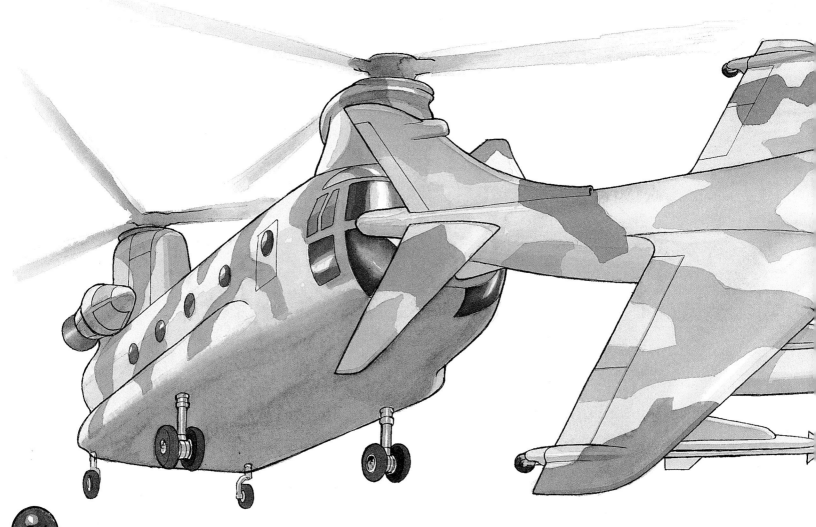

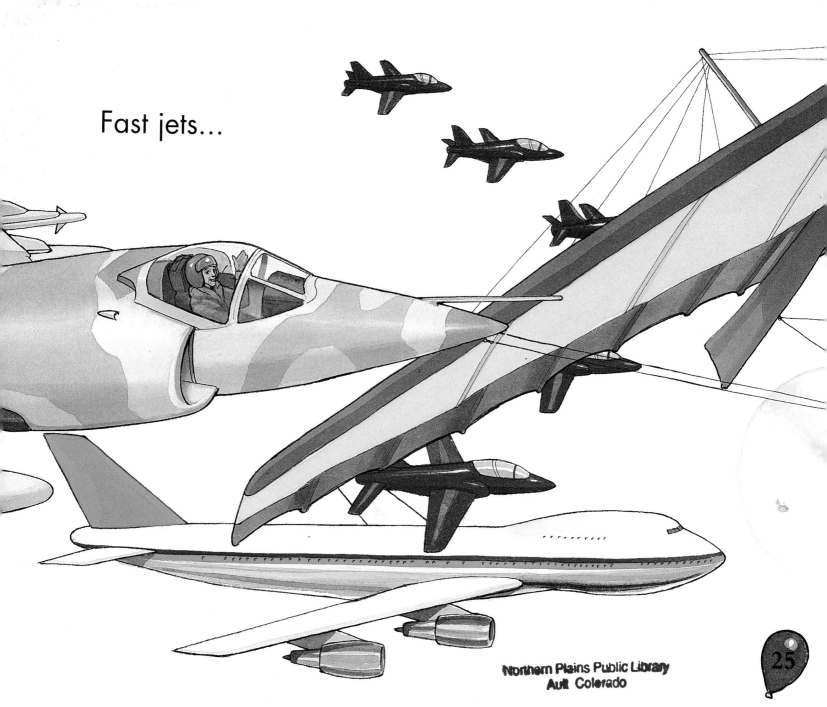

Fast jets...

25

Slower ultralight...

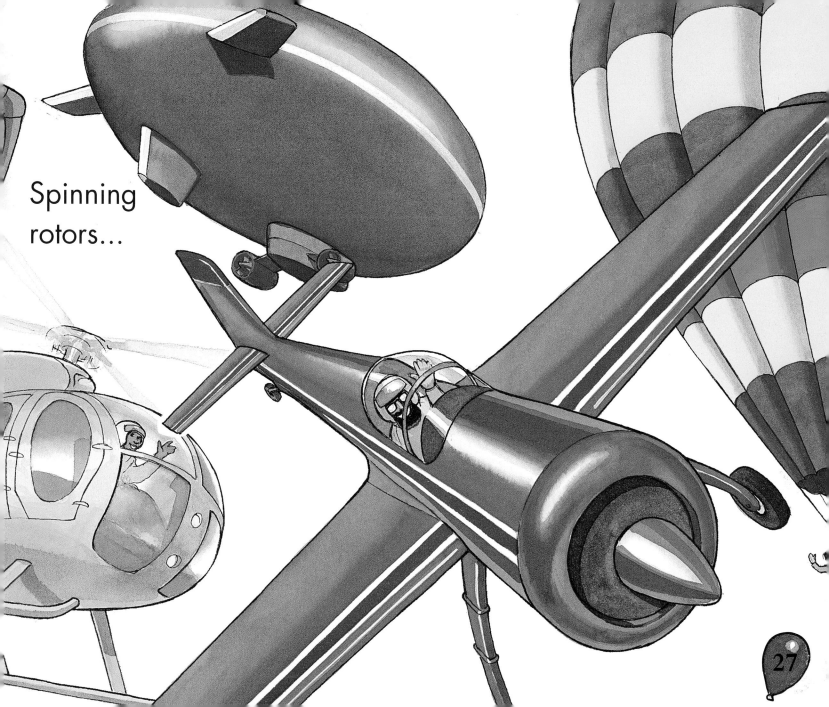

Spinning
rotors...

All fly away!

28

INTERESTING FACTS...

- The first creatures to fly were a rooster, duck, and sheep. They went up in a hot-air balloon, in 1783!
- The first airplane flight with a passenger lasted 29 seconds, in 1908!
- A jet engine moves a plane by a jet of gases moving fast!
- A Boeing 747 "jumbo jet" is the biggest passenger jet in the world. Some can carry 600 people!
- Besides people, a jumbo jet can carry a lot of luggage and packages. The "hold" can carry the weight of 12 large elephants!
- The U.S. President flies in a special Boeing 747 called "Air Force One."

GLOSSARY

airship an aircraft lighter than air that can be steered

biplane an airplane with two sets of wings, one over the other

Concorde the world's fastest passenger plane

daredevil a reckless person doing dangerous tricks

hang glider a large kind of kite that a person flies

helicopter a small aircraft going straight up, with spinning blades

hot-air balloon a large balloon filled with hot air and a basket below

jumbo jet a very large jet plane, carrying many people

jump jet a fixed wing jet that can take-off straight up

loops-the-loop turning a plane in the air, making curved rings

parachute a cloth-like umbrella opened when someone jumps from a plane, to slow fall

sky divers people jumping from an airplane, doing tricks

ultralight a small private fun plane

INDEX